World Stage Press

Verse from the Village

DEATH BY COMB

DEATH BY COMB

A COLLECTION OF POETRY BY

Camari Carter

11/3/17

World Stage Press
Verse from the Village

World Stage Press
Verse from the Village

Layout Design by Nadia Hunter Bey
Cover Design by Undeniable Ink
Copy Editing by Marilyn Forrest

To the relentless Matriarchs who formed me:
You've led – and, this is me following. Thank you
for lighting the way.

Mom (Melinda Lewis)
Gramma (Agnes Young)
Granny (Evalena Carter)

TABLE OF CONTENTS

FORWARD BY WILLIAM HAWKINS

God has pulled Camari Carter from the soil. She did not put up a fighter neither was her seed cast on a footpath or shallow soil. This poet was tucked deep like stories in the belly of our cherished griots or hymns underneath our Baptist pews. There was no worry about the darkness that surrounded her or the harsh conditions waiting above ground.

Her first book "Death By Comb" is a resilient and authentic literary offering that bears its petals without shame. Now her time has come to be presented; for her creation and splendor to be admired by the world. These pages move like the seasons. Winds of tragedy have pushed her; the sun has bitten at her patience. Betrayal falls at her feet like a thousand flowers; she picks them up one by one. Her stories will hang in your heart and sing like a summer's sunset. This published work proves that her stems are still vulnerable, but proud and deeply rooted.

Carter is an author who deserves the praise for which she is due. Her works will turn over the stones of our rigid beliefs. Her metaphors will draw us in like the pose of a honeysuckle, and her depth is as brilliant as the head of a sunflower. "Death By Comb" has carried her stories like a rose bears its thorns. She is protected. Her beauty and works are something we should hold with caution and cherish forever. We have come to behold the treasure of God and humanity at this garden, through the writings of our sister, author, friend, and truth-teller, Camari Carter.

William Hawkins
Founder of Art Is Forever Non-profit
Author of "Feta Cheese Jesus", a collection of poems
Los Angeles, CA

A WORD FROM DENNIS CRUZ

Death by Comb, the debut collection of poetry by Camari Carter, sparkles like eyes gleaming from the shadows of an unlit street. At once fragile and stoic, her poems weave a tapestry that traverses her emotional landscape with deft and brevity, but never at the expense of her authenticity. By navigating the expanse of her experience, her work belies a tenderness that is not immediately apparent as she faces the struggles of a spirit caught in the snares of the human condition. Issues of gender, race, mortality, love and loss, are handled with grace and unflinching candor. Never succumbing to the trappings of a cliché or melodrama, Camari's poems take the reader on a perilous journey of pain and discovery, offering no guarantee of safety. Wearing her scars like badges of courage, it is evident that her poems stand, not just as testimonies to the hardships of being, but as proclamations of survival and victory.

At once vulnerable and confrontational, Death by Comb is Carter's answer to the questions that plague us all. Why are we here? What is love? How do we survive? Resolute in her response to the existential crisis that lives in the heart of every artist, Carter never cowers from the possibility that perhaps there is no answer.

It is Ms. Carter's willingness to brave the dark, despite the obvious perils, that lend her work its pulse, and this book is a testament to the strength of its heartbeat.

-Dennis Cruz
Author of Moth Wing Tea

INTRODUCTION

There are specific times in our lives when life seems to use all of its tools to hammer away every bit of hope, love, and fight in you. Then, there are also times when a great fight arises in us. Those bruises and scars seem to hurt less because every bit of strength in you is used to overcome.

Welcome to my fight.

Death by Comb is by far a body of work that stands near my heart as I explored a time in my life when I realized that I was fragile. I could be broken. This book was written during that period. You are indeed reading my heart, pain, and triumph distilled through my pen and now into your hands.

I only ask one favor of you.

Please read from start to finish. I want to take you through a journey. I hope you can keep up.

Wheels up!

Camari

DEATH BY COMB

"I choose to reflect the times and the situations in which I find myself. That to me is my duty."

- Nina Simone

(from the documentary, *What Happened, Miss Simone?*)

Good Morning,

to the person I should've been,
the ideas, fresh like hung linen in September
the future; my affair with the past kept
my eyes off of you
good morning,
to the courage mantled on my shoulders
the bountiful love resting on my skin
I let it permeate my veins
let it become me
good morning, a new day

Love Still
to William

We met at an open mic that winter night
The wind-chill made me wear
a snug pink sweater
and tights as thick as the clouds that hung low
ready like the moon waiting all day for her turn;
to sing, to glisten, and to awaken the night.
It was something special;
I knew something special would happen.

The rug I sat on didn't cushion my bum
or protect it
from the concrete
but the pain didn't matter because
his voice proved
heaven was real.
His voice laid feathery light on my ears
his voice convinced me
love still had a song
I loved him right away

I believed his fingers were touching God
instead of the guitar.
His singing sounded like
angels chanting
joining in the chorus
I'm sure it was a divine interaction-
a prophecy, even

that love
would still find a way to the broken places
love still found a way to me.

The Fear List

1. I fear I will try "chitlins" and like them
2. I fear I'd marry someone
with the same name as mine and on our wedding
night, I'd be scared to scream out his – or my name,
and enjoy it narcissistically
3. I fear I'd be entrapped in a room full of unglazed
donuts, and I'd have to eat my way out, without
anything to drink,
except unflavored, sparkling water
4. I fear to drink OJ without pulp
5. Milk without Oreos
6. Drinking water from a cup with soap suds in it
7. Plain, unsalted, un-honeyed roasted peanuts
8. I fear having to drive 13 miles to work on E, and
I'm already 15 minutes late
9. I fear men's feet in thong sandals
10. Women's feet unpainted or,
dangling over open-toed stilettos
11. I fear my own feet sans lotion
12. Cell phone battery on 1% and I have 70% GPS
directions left
13. I fear patterned clothing
14. Ankle pants on women taller than 5"8.'
15. A weave with tight, painful braids
16. Wearing a wig while walking
in high-speed winds

17. I fear sitting next to a smelly person on a 5-hour flight, with no layovers, and I am in the window seat – trapped by his force field of funk
18. I fear eye boogers
19. Unfilled eyebrows
20. Too thick eyebrows
21. Barely there eyebrows
22. I fear DTPWB – Donald Trump as President while Black

There are many things I fear,
but none trumps my fear of the Lord.
The one who created this earth with just a baby's breath whisper, who forgave me with one flicker of his thoughts.
The one who keeps me
from abandoning this jungle-gymed life,
he leads me gently
does not frighten
but gives me peace

I fear to lose a love like that.

Frisbee

I panted
at your feet
begged
for a drip of you
I was a good girl
pulled out all the tricks
rolled,
jumped,
when you commanded.
licked your ego,
waited
in your absence.
I welcomed your return sweetly.
You were the Frisbee,
back and forth you came.
I chased after you
further and further
you flew away,
and I could never catch you

Broken Promise

Disappointment from a broken promise
sticks around too long.
It is the out of town relative
who overstays his welcome
doesn't know when to go home.
It is that long, awkward silence
after a failed joke.
A lingering feeling
providing company to your grief.
It brings to the party its best friends-
remorse and dejection.
You want them to leave
yet, want them to stay
to fill the void and
the promise
left emptied.

Questions You Do Not Ask A Black Woman –Pt 1.

There are three hundred and
sixty-six thousand,
one hundred and fifty-six
questions,
you should never ask a black woman:

1. Is that your hair?

2. Is it real?

3. Can I touch it?

4. Why does it feel that way?

5. Why doesn't mine do that?

6. That's a weave, huh?

7. Why do you need a weave?

8. Is it true you all are always mad?

9. What is it like to be black?

Diana

Tender and fragile
unblemished skin and tiny body
a yellow mooned face
smile brighter than the noon
Diana, Diana
stumbled into my class
quieter than a night of camping
faintest two year old I've ever seen
with dirty, stuck-on-scalp, corn silk hair
wearing the same filth-stained pink pants
she wore all week
Diana
smelled of un-kept -
a pissy, sewage stench
that remained in your nose
hours after cradling her,
never let me change a diaper
or hug her.
Diana
a peculiar, observant child.
While others enjoyed
worn out tonka's and dolls,
Diana stood solemnly
fingers intertwined like distant lovers
unwilling to leave each other again.
Diana
didn't want to go home,
at the sight of momma and poppa,

classmates drop toys
crayons
even cookies to leave
But not Diana.
Soon she'd gained my trust,
allowed me to wash away smut
from toddler-sized arms and legs
playground dirt from yesterday
she'd come in with every morning.
Diana
I wish I knew sooner,
should've known when
I saw how you'd try to protect
your teensy-weensy body
not let anyone touch you
Your indifference to playing,
or eat chocolate chips
color in red to heart-shaped lines
unwillingness to run in the sand
resistance to mimic moooooooooooos and
naaaaaaaaattts.
Diana
when I changed your diaper;
sprinkled soothing baby powder,
I saw openness between your chubby legs
too young to be thighs, yet
I saw damage to your girlhood;
forced into womanhood.
The slit area
much like a heat split baked potato.
An open Ziploc snack bag,

you didn't want me to change you
afraid I'd be like your Dad.
Diana
I saw him look at you, salivating
with hunger, only a wolf could have.
I watched you walk
slowly
towards the door when he came for you.
Maybe
you thought he'd probe inside of you again,
interrupt your sweet sleep,
maybe you thought you'd never come back to class
where you felt safe.
But, baby
I couldn't protect you
that was supposed to be a father's job
to guard you against the monster he turned out to
be.

The Dream and The Chaser

I'm running,
trying to move faster
but my soul has prosthetics
I'm limping
dragging my wounded passion
and what's left of my belief!
But, the weight of this lack,
this void
where my dreams should be
is an open dome
without a team to play
it all lays heavy on my back
like bowling balls
and I can't spare another day
in this same place
This.   Same.   Place.
Stuck like a fat rat on a sticky mat
I feel like
I'm held back on the wrists
by two dream killers
they're snarling at me
I'm swinging, belligerently
forcing my way up
like I'm drowning in a frozen lake
I'm pushing
I've got to breathe
I got to reach that dream
and it's as far as God's shoulder

past the clouds
past the universe
and I'm going to reach it
even if my whole body blows to pieces
and I have a hand left
let that hand be a cyborg
walk on fingertips
til it jumps
and catches my dream.

My Relationship With HER

We hooked up 11 years ago. I met her at a high point in my life. Just graduated high school, single, an official adult; the perfect time. I got drunk with the idea of college, and, heck, she had money. We flirted in letters. She offered a couple of years of independence, growth, and adventure. So, we got married. With no hesitation, I signed the papers. We were rolling. For four years, she gave me money, freedom, and adventure. But, just like any woman, she wasn't going to let me live off of her for too long. About six months after I graduated college, she had her hand out. Waiting for me to pay out, but I was cash out and ass out. I promised her that one day my degree would be worth it. I would land a high-paying job with benefits, and it'd be my turn to take care of her. Seven years later, she and I have been off and on. She called it forbearance. I bared four different jobs, in four years and still couldn't afford to pay this chick back. Someone, please, just write me a big, fat check, so I can finally divorce Sallie Mae Department of Education, NelNet, Direct Loans, Navient, or whatever she's calling herself nowadays.

Morning Prayer

awaken my senses
may I see good ole days
while living them.
smell their goodness
taste laughter
feel their sunshine kissing my neck,
and hear them whispering moments to keep.
May I maximize precious seconds
so when regret knocks on my door,
I won't answer.

TV Hair vs. My Hair

That moment when I realized
I didn't have Tracee Ellis Ross' hair ...
you know her,
Diana Ross' daughter
Girlfriend's TV Show
Black-ish – *her*.
My most monumental moment ever;
I remember it like it was yesterday
when I decided to go on this "heatless" hair
challenge.
That's when I realized
I didn't have Tracee Ellis Ross' hair,
Tia and Tamera Mowry's hair,
Alicia Keys' hair,
or any of those ladies with "loose tresses."
I started off watching You-Tube videos
and all of those girls led me astray
telling me to
try this
twist that
do this
braid that
my hair never quite turned out like theirs.
I even went as far as trying one of those "wash and
go's."
That's when you simply wash – and – go…
I was so confident that
I bought all the "right" products

those girls told me to get,
but my wash and go
was a wash and stop.
More like a stay and pray
because I wasn't going anywhere
with the way my hair turned out!
My Tracee Ellis Ross,
Alicia Keys,
Tia and Tamera Mowry dreams
turned into a Miss Ceelie-
"you told Harpo to beat me" nightmare.
My coily strands began to hug each other closely
my "once" drenched hair
quickly turned dry and dull
the springs in my hair were sprung
and with all of that washing
it looked like I've done nothing.

I remember staring into the mirror saying
"My hair is so ugly" and cried that ugly cry.
You know that cry
when you can't differentiate
tears, saliva, and snot
determined not to give up – I reached for my
artillery – the comb
my hair resisted movement like a stubborn child
I tried to appease my hair
like a parent with an unruly child
tries anything to get her to obey
brush, water, gel, hell – even juices and berries
my hair still didn't comply

But – alas – a lopsided afro
I felt subconscious about my hair
as I went to work at an attorney's office
my feelings validated
as those unrelated to me
by any means
reached out to touch
and I leaned back like it's a game of limbo
Hell no, you can't touch my hair!
Don't you know I just came out of the battlefield
barely alive with this hair?
Don't you know the soldiers of my combs gave
their lives for this mission today?
My causalities alone
this week was
three combs
eight hair clips
and 15 scrunchies.
So Please,
save me the agony
save the questions for someone else
because it's unfair
it's unfair that I took the opinions and
specifications
everyone else had about my hair
and made them into a Bible.
If my hair is too tightly coiled – I need a hot comb
but if it resembles
Brazilian, Malaysian
Indian, Mongolian
Peruvian

anything but African,
it's considered exotic.
If my bad hair day looks like a style
that should be seen in the remake of
Roots, The Color Purple
Amistad, and Rosewood,
I should slap on a wig because it's not professional
and "I shouldn't let these people see me like this."
Like what?
Who I really am?
Well, this is what I have to say to those who don't
want me for who I am

Silence

I won't waste another day
another hour
or another second pleading my case for you
or even myself, to see
my hair is brilliant
yes, it is dull
that's because my soul radiates enough
yes, you can't comb through my hair
without elbow grease
but, that's not for you to worry
yes, you can't easily run your fingers through my
hair
because you're not supposed to touch it anyway.
It's stiff because it is art

it stays in place
for you to gasp and marvel at
how it resembles a field of floral wonder
so no, it will not blow in the wind
that's how trees break
my hair is tough
durable
strong
unbreakable
it is like me
so that moment I realized
I didn't have Tracee Ellis Ross' hair
was the moment I said
I'd rather have mine.

Moles

There are parts of my grandmother on my skin
chocolate deposits
small, random collections of memories.
Passed down from generations.
Every day, another one appears,
by looking, I can recount
the events of each day
each mole is a time capsule
I can refer to,
to remember the times I loved
remember the times my grandmother laughed
the time she mourned
the day I made her proud
I connect the dots
and they form the word;
beauty

Mia's Dream

Mia saw God in the form of a dream. She was drifting in a sea of difficult decisions, and it was time for her to choose a fish. She needed to relocate, and this thought alone plagued her. In the dream, God showed her a lush, green fern growing from a pot. Then, he said, "In the morning, I want you to look up why a plant should be repotted."
The next morning, Mia tended to Google and commenced her search. The article said plants should be repotted because they have outgrown their pot and needed a larger space to grow further. However, if the plant is not repotted, it will grow roots surrounding the entire pot. At this point, the only way to remove the plant is to forcefully pull it out and hit the bottom of the pot.
After reading the article, Mia realized that God was gently guiding her to growth. Then, she made her decision to move on.
God does not always seek flashing lights, burning bushes, and fireworks to speak. It is when we are still. It is in the mundane, beautiful moments we are gently guided.

I Just Don't
a haiku from the mind of all girls with barely-there Dads

I know who you are
I'm not fatherless; I just
don't know who you *are*.

Haunted Nursery Rhyme

one kick
two kick
three kick
floor!

momma grabs her belly
to protect from more.

1 punch
2 grabs
3 slaps
run!

momma grabs big sister
runs from the gun

out the door
down the steps
on the grass
now!

there's a crowd forming
heard the screams get loud

get in the car
get in the car
get in the car
hide!

the neighbor tries to protect us
we didn't go on a ride

get out the car
get out the car
get out the car
Bitch!

Mommy's boyfriend yells
but Mommy didn't flinch.

soon she got out
and went with him
I was all alone!

would Mommy come back
would a baby be in the belly
I sat on the steps and cried.

The night grew dark
they came back
my fears quieted a little

but he never left
I prayed he would
his presence still haunts me

Victim and the Passerby

The moment I laid eyes on her wet eyes I knew.
Her eyes spoke an unknown language, yet
I understood it
Silently, she screamed for me
to be her hero
save her from this villain boyfriend
her eyes screamed anguish,
shrieked confusion.
Hands, once warm turned to cold rock
eyes once in love, now in hate
palms once open and healing,
now closed and hurting
mouth, once for sweet kisses
beautiful blessings
turned to biting and curses.
I sensed the questioning in her eyes.
A scientist can tell you how a liquid turns into a gas
But, who can tell you
How love can turn sour?
Who can provide enough reason to stay?
A reminisce in her eyes
validated the reason
remembering kind moments
I felt her fears of staying
and leaving
they weighed on the scales of her heart,
she always stayed
waiting for him to change.

But, it was her that did.
Her heart,
once passionately red
beaten black and blue
cinnamon brown eyes
swollen shut
kissable lips
now untouchable
I was just a passerby
in those few seconds, our eyes met
I flashbacked to my very own moment.
His once-sweet words
turned bitter
a nightmare that I couldn't wake up from
he believed to be helping me,
but his words
were empty deposits
into an already overdraft soul;
a bloodthirsty cycle of
me giving
him taking.

I related to this woman
Now, she my past, and I her future
I hope the language from my eyes
echoed hope during bleak times,
empowerment when weak
courage to walk away
When fear crept in to make her stay.
Light when everything is dark
Jesus when the enemy seeks to destroy her.

Because it is He, that took a beating,
so she or anyone else wouldn't have to.

Heaviness

I go to sleep every night
expecting a difference in the morning
but it's not there.
Gramma said joy came by
but I must have still been asleep
or snoozed too many times.
Now I'm rushing to catch up
wiping the wet residue off my face
I look at my pillow
only to find weeds
from the tears I sowed last night,
my ground too hard
too long
still struggling to break through
this concrete mass
seemingly sprawled over my garden
The weeds of my mind
seemed to have come through my ears
to my neck;
choking the life out of me
I'm just praying
I am heard
hoping I'm not too far
nor distant from God in this forest
created by my fears.
The weeds
then tie up my ankles
I fight to break through

and I feel dumped into a sea of sadness.
It all started with one problem
I felt I could fix alone.
But I couldn't and
that led to two
added four
multiplied by ten more
which is how I landed on the sea's floor
Alone
Lost
Stuck
taking steps despite the despair of my mind
But going nowhere.
Like being on a merry go round
thinking I'm moving past something
when I've actually gone nowhere
I want to find my path,
my purpose

Unmentionable Revolutionaries

Revolutionaries don't always wear combat boots.
The ones I see
probably don't know what those are
or would prefer sandals
showing off bright pink
painted toes
or light-up tennis shoes.

The revolutionaries I know
stay up late preparing songs
to drastically transform the way
we all think of love
they encourage everyone else
while emotionally decaying inside
They deplete life savings to open
a non-profit for at-risk kids,
or to just follow their heart.
The married revolutionaries
violently rebelling
our heavy divorce society
using passion as guns and love as bullets
proving monogamy is still desirable

I know revolutionaries the height
of grocery carts
Standing up to bullies
Some of who work on part-time jobs
to fund their full-time art.

Revolutionaries
deserted wealthy, vocational careers
Mom and Dad wanted for them
and embraced the gravel-laden road
of art
or to travel the world,
or just to seek out their own
whatever it may be.
People who devote their life
only to a calling;
only to the light in themselves

Untreated

I always thought death was distant and neglected
Now it is as close as my blouse
sitting across from my doctor
my tears anxiously awaited
their nose dives onto my dress
when she said
Camari, if you leave your thyroid untreated, you'll
die.

Last month, she said I was almost normal
that's when I reached for herbals
my earthquake levels quieted
my Tracee Ellis' like bug eyes retreated into their
shells
weakened and shaky hands
then, allowed me to open water bottles
although, I enjoyed my plummeted weight
I didn't look sick and sunken
my insomnia surrendered, and I slept

However, this doctor
had a disdain for herbal remedies
insisted I trade them for pharms
she, sounding a lot like Charlie Brown
whomp whomp
whomp whomp
whomp
I listened

as this woman
concluded my life as if she commenced it

I shook with naked emotions
plunged into her iced lake of words
as she threatened the vitality of my womb
a tree with no fruit
potential desert hill
miscarriages of my future offspring
kids that already have names
kids that already have last names
kids that already had names I made up before this
appointment

Her words ripped the pink paper
with the list of my future children
two boys, two girls

My options limited to chalky white circles
radioactive concoctions
an incision in my lower neck
scraping the remaining of this organ

She offered a "cure" that came with more
harmful effects
like the commercial advertising a new drug
"Are you suffering? Take this pill for relief.
Side effects include:
Sleeplessness
Fatigue
Loss of vision

Panic attacks
Difficulty breathing
Diarrhea
Nausea
Vomiting
Suicide ideations
Liver problems
Kidney stones
Muscle weakness
Difficulty in walking
Difficulty in seeing
Difficulty in pissing
High blood pressure
Low blood pressure
Barely alive pressure
Nose bleeds
Ear bleeds
Toe bleeds
Butt bleeds
The whole body bleeds.

I've jealously compared my structured life to those
living carelessly, and
I just can't shake this misunderstanding of life
cautiously lived
and this is my reward.

The Promise

In my lap laid a preciously plump baby boy
peaceful in my arms,
his face reflected my own
prominent ancient nose,
full African lips,
the tone of a peeled yellow nectarine,
features prominently detailed
like God personally
carved this tiny prince
just for me
our glances locked in wonderment
I wanted to hold him in my arms
until they fell numb;
I'd simply lay facing heaven
with him on my chest in rest and prayer
I did not want to lose sight of him, yet
I'd awakened to morning,
a solemn room
unlit
My prince vanished with the dream.
he still
left me with a note from God saying
he is my promise,
an antidote to counteract
doctoral predictions of a defective womb
after all,
they are just practicing
while God is perfecting

Dreams

are child-like and fragile
guard them with bubble-wrapped prayers
secure them from shattering falls and thieves
once broken,
it can take years to repair
or replace entirely

in youthful age,
dreams are overpopulated dandelion fields
pick a dream
any dream
blow it into existence

in aged years,
dreams are fathers who never leave their family
rare and desired
interrupted by the adult necessity
duty
delay
impatience
a giving-up
a decline in strength
listening to voices of reasoning

Dreams are non-negotiable.
they are proof of our purpose
the purpose that drives us
keeps us breathing

many discard them with leftovers
but, we must remember
they are child-like, fragile, rare
we must guard them with bubble-wrapped prayers
once broken
it can take years to repair
or replace entirely

A Lonely Place

I wish I could have a more spiritual, faith-filled response to bad news. I do not have a good track record for staying afloat on positivity in a bowl of uncertainty; especially, when that bowl widens to Olympic sized.

I experienced a lonely place in my car, with a note in hand from a doctor stating a decline in my health. My lonely place advanced to a field of trees where I considered joining the characters in Nina Simone's "Strange Fruit."

Then, I reached for my phone to make a call; looking for some aloe words to my scorched hope. I was only left with a tainted mantra "it's not that deep," and a text with a sad face emoji. My threats to harm myself did not warrant a call, a prayer, a hug, or a conversation over coffee to calm my rage. I felt as if my empowerment and faith ran off to Paris to enjoy pasta and wine than to weather this hell with me. Yet, in my lowest, faintest, darkest moment, I never felt God abandon me in my loneliness. There is warmth, a resounding calm that soothes, right at the last second. That is when I know I'm closest to God. Maybe, that is where I'm supposed to be.

Mother? May I?
For the women desiring motherhood

many chilly mornings
when frost collected at the tip of my nose
I arise
waltz to the restroom
and to the mirror
I stick out my belly
wishing on twinkled stars
teething rings
onesies
pretending to be expecting.
I rub my desired magic eight ball tummy
imagine the floating, white triangle
granting me a baby
I see that triangle mold into a square crib
then, a square home
where my family will grow
my husband will lead
and always love
it is these daydreams
these longings
mental holograms
that push me past
maybe's
can we's
can I's
these realistic dreams are the fuel
that lets me know
motherhood will soon be mine

Closeted
a haiku

I am your closet
unload your burdens in me
close my door, then leave

Wine
a poem for those standing in celibacy

I wish I never met you
you and other men
who think my toffee-coated
coca-cola shaped bottle body
will allow you to plaster your hands
on my cap
twist so you can taste
thinking my sparkling dark
can be ladled for you to gulp.
My cap is sealed tightly,
withstanding a few tears
from greedy hands that obeyed commands of
thirsty stomachs.
They grabbed my bottle and shook.
As I tried to resist,
my sparkles began to rise
reacting from touches and pulls
bubbles surfaced
laced with lust
bubbles wanted to release
as fingers gripped curves.
For years,
I've worked on settling these bubbles
protecting my cap
I wish I never met you.
I let your hands
slightly tear my seal

knowing your palms held lines of theft,
lips murderous
I resisted your caresses
and the rise of my insides
But, I'll never compromise
because in His eyes
I am wine
aged-to-perfection
savored by a godly man
who will appreciate the wait

V – Piece
dedicated to those who have waited and still are

I am still a virgin
There, I said it!
I felt like I had to keep that secret for years.
It was like I had
a don't ask
don't tell
policy about my sexuality
when in reality
It's something I should talk about boldly
Well, after countless relationship rejections
because I couldn't
more like wouldn't
relieve their erections,
I figured I'd keep it on hush
I thought
maybe
if I stayed quiet about it,
it would buy me more time
for a guy to see my heart
fall in love with me
instead with what was in between.

Silence never brought me anything but shame
just being afraid to claim
that the reason
for my quest for purity is all for the one
with the purest name

I was scared to carry my cross
afraid to be different
afraid of more rejection
So instead of being OUTstanding
I chose to WITHstand
stand with him who pressured me
quite inadvertently
calling me wifey
oh that word wifey
just a cover up term that just really means
free booty without accountability
I wondered,
is sex the only love that I can show?
He said, If you love me you'd do this
If I don't, I must hate you
How could my choice to wait
equate with hate?

I thought he would understand.
We were both Christians
But I guess
devotion to Christ
should only be displayed
on Sunday mornings
and not with my body
on Saturday nights
The time he said he would wait for me
must have meant just a couple of weeks.
I never understood
how a word like "virgin" could
make men cringe

maybe because being with one
would really test their strength.

Sometimes I fear of becoming
a 40-year-old virgin
living in a sex-driven society
that no longer honors celibacy
but considers it a mockery
rather saddens me.

This wasn't always my plan.
My frustration
with shallow guys
who would only want one part of me
resulted in my way
of sifting for one
who could really
want
just
me.

Plant
a haiku

the living room plant
forgotten, dry, and withered
we are much alike

MISSING!!

MISSING!!

Has anyone seen her? She strayed away last night.
I've been looking in streets and alleyways, and
there is no trace of her. I shouldn't have kept her
locked in for so long without room to flourish. She
may be with someone else who's really taking good
care of her. Those types don't wait for you to grow
into an owner. They need you to be ready.
If you see my Dreams, tell her that I've been
looking for her.
Tell her to come home.
I'm ready now.

A Pianist's Cry
A theatrical monologue response to unmet expectations

The speaker plays 30-second intro of Clair de Lune on piano stops to speak

I wanted to be a classical concert pianist
same desire as Nina Simone,
yet, I followed a different path
that stopped abruptly.
I didn't become the lawyer I studied to be
I am sorry I failed you.
You wanted something I couldn't be.
I see the disdain in your eyes
when you look at me
when you tell your friends what I really do
how I really make my money
where I really live
how I'm unlike what you thought, I'd be
I'm unlike who I thought I'd be

*the speaker continues with Clair de Lune on piano
the speaker continues to talk while playing a tune*

I've failed myself,
so you can't fail me
I let everyone tell me who I am,
and ought to be

I've abandoned my dream
let a nobody tell me
no one wanted to stand in line
just to see me sit down and play piano
   Why did I listen?
Let her talk me out of the only passion
the only, original dream
I've given myself
I play better than Alicia Keys
I could duet with John Legend
I didn't mean to be naïve…
just needed someone to believe in me

music heightens

instead, I was raped raw of my innocence
My future; I am empty
Yet… I have 2 degrees
You can tell everyone about that!
Don't forget to mention that no one will hire me
overeducated   underemployed
over-indebted   under self-esteemed
over-aged   underpaid
why does everyone turn to me for help
and I'm left turning into walls

heightened music begins to settle

where does a creative fit into this black and white
world
where you are expected to break
cram into tight spaces
I am too large for this conveyor belt
Please accept my weighty
I'm heavy
understand I am different from you

Death by Comb

I comb
rake
groom
scrape
separate
tease, and untangle
more than my hair
the peculiarities of my personality
odd infatuations,
with detangling
the sound of my voice
I want to use this bristled tool
to run,
and slice its way
through this evergreen forest
shrubbery of this need
for others to tell me what to think
I want this comb to take pieces of me I repulse,
with the rest of the shedding
Let the worry,
teary regrets,
and the unforgiven
be gathered in the rake
fisted
then, tossed alongside old Q – Tips
and dirty towels
I want to fine tooth myself
until all kinks and knots

have been mercilessly snatched out
until there's nothing left of me.

It's Easy

10th floor
of a Houston hotel,
veins quiver,
muscles prepare
for flight.
A simple move
the ground floor
calls me,
my mind
pressuring me
gently persuading
it's easy
just jump

Bomb

I am a ticking time bomb with 2 seconds left
a sensitive device
with the tiniest touch of a rat's whisper
a boiled egg's shell
after its plunge in cold water
I will break
crumble in your hands
make your life a mess
like a toddler's first taste of a cake
An unfinished puzzle
spilling flour near a fan on high speed.
If you touch me
if your eyes shift towards me
I will explode
like the soda can left in the freezer
a balloon out of patience
tread very softly

Diseased Feeling

It is that nightmare when a monster, ravenous dog, or a snake is chasing you, and you know you are running faster than an Olympian, but you're running in place.

It is using your last few dollars to stock your refrigerator, then your lights get turned off.

It is sleeping a full 8 hours, and feeling as though you had none.

It is getting out of bed only to fall to the floor as if someone has thrown a 5-year-old on your back.

It feels as if your veins carry heavy whipping cream and with each moment, you are brimmed full and slowed.

It has everyone telling you to exercise and eat right, and you have been for years.

It is trying desperately to find someone to understand your Turkish Language in Ghana.

It is doing all of the right things to improve, heal, push, further yourself and you realize, you've gone nowhere.

Afraid To Love You

I am not afraid to love you
Well, I am afraid to love you
I am standing on this shore
all I want to do
is put my feet in
test the waters
I hear you say
Jump in, the water's fine!
The truth is, I know it's fine
It has been fine
I'm afraid it's too fine
If I jump into your water
I'll never swim back to land
I will swim so deep,
just to drown in you
without fighting
let your love engulf me
let it seep through every part of me
inhale you
in my lungs, bronchi
every cavity
would be filled with you
parts of you would travel my bloodstream
landing at my heart
I'll want to leave you there
I'll swim to the deepest of your heart
see wonders
exclusive VIP wonders

like how you give for the sake of giving
your integrity when no one's watching
earnest worship of God
no one sees
or the tears worn on your face like veils
emotions you reveal
unearthing deepest fears
entrusting them to me
but some of your wonders are intimidating
the storms you've cried while anxiously waiting
just to touch your dreams
or from the sting of cuts
left by those who left you
you don't hold back
and you show me all

I'm afraid to love you
not for what I've seen
but from what you'll see
in my ocean
Will you still love me
during my hurricane season
that comes once a month?
a category 5
emotions disastrous if untamed
indecisive, moody, feisty
all of this anchored
down to my ocean's floor
and I'll want you to leave them there
but you – fearless and inquisitive
the drive of your love will push you

deeper into my Bermuda
deeper into who I really am

that's why I am afraid to love you
because, you want all of me,
and I want all of you.

Marks and Movies
A little recount of Gramma's birthplace

I don't think Gramma liked watching The Butler
It was hard watching it with her

I'd have to sit thru her comments and recounts of
Marks, Mississippi
where she picked blackberries in the forest
where her father farmed vegetables
chopped wood and sold them for pennies.
Her Mother
canned those vegetables and fruit
and taught her children to do the same

A town where Gramma learned to be quiet
never complain when her teacher
would beat her other peers
couldn't yell as she saw
their skin like chocolate congos tremble
and shiver with each whipping
She learned to keep secrets
and that "no " and "stop" was never to come from
her mouth

I think it was hard for her to watch The Butler
a reminder of the times when she was
almost-human
almost-speak up
almost-have a life of your own

almost-live in peace
The constant tearing in her human seams

Gramma related to The Butler
She too, A Butler at 21 for some Jews
She hates telling this story,
how she worked for half a penny
worked her fingers bare raisin
in exchange for humiliating pay
how she witnessed Ms. Lady and her husband fight
Flying ceramic plates,
quilted napkins soaring like softballs
Gramma ignored it,
never suited up to break up the fight
Lady asked Gramma,
"Na, why you didn't say anything? Ya just stood
there?"
Gramma said, "What was I supposed to do?"

Gramma knew better
She breaks up that fight,
it might as well had been her fight

The Butler reminds Gramma of her past
I try to remind her
I am the reward of her sacrifice
every chance I have
to listen and recount her life
is an honest history lesson
I'll never want to miss

What Is It Like To Be Black?

My white roommate
asked me what it was like to be black.

I quickly stopped coloring
brown in Ariel, the Disney-ed mermaid's, lines
I was in the middle of creating a cartoon
I could relate to
and get interrupted with this question,
too deep,
too invasive,
too confusing for me,
a girl from South Central
who never interacted
personally,
with white people until college,
to answer.
This question upset me
I didn't think I'd ever have to explain my culture to
someone completely oblivious
this question saddened me
she knew little about black people

She asked me what it was like to be black,
in which I answered:

Black is the color of pressure
A pressing, withstanding
The color of survival and comebacks

Suffer
We are blamed – too quickly
Killed – mercilessly
Underpaid
Untrusted
Muted
swept under welcome mats
America's step children
misunderstood
orphans
invisible
dismissed
yet, We are the creators
Unstoppable
Originators
Envied
copied from
Rich
Brimming with laughter
resourceful
colorful
culture
Innovative
Avant- Garde
Royalty

My answer to a question I thought
I'd never have to answer
an answer that satisfied and disturbed
an answer that left her regretful for asking

yet, she had a genuine longing to understand

I never apologized for my abruptness
because I felt my description true
I am only left with the guilt of impatience
in an opportunity to peacefully explain
How the lack of my cultural representation in
mainstream media leaves white people to ask
unreasonable questions.
I don't have to ask anything about her
her culture is overly saturated on television,
in malls,
grocery stores,
and freeway marketing.
Her question represented
the mass ignorance of black culture,
and that is what upset me.
.
However, at 17 years old,
I didn't have the capacity to say all of this.

Police Hunt

Dust cannons into the air
tarnished bullet capsules
land onto the ground like dog scraps
war-like sounds
sliced through the thickness of silence
a young man runs loosely
his dodges failed
like they did in middle school
tiny metal intruders
force their way into his skin
blood bursts from his roundness
his footsteps, a drunkard's waltz,
he retreats to a nearby porch
no rest, no iced lemonade
no sweet chats of last summer
only a cascade of thoughts
that persuade him
to consider
death as his only escape route
Suddenly,
black and blue crowd him
they sing a melancholic Miranda lament
and capture him
invite him to see their cage
to stay for a while
while viewers watch it all
on the Fox News
on a warm, Saturday afternoon.

Dear MSN Journalists,

sings
You may think that I am
quiet
meek
hidden
You may see this gentle giant

You may think that I will
tremble
shiver
crumble

But what you don't know
What you can't see
What is beneath is a
Queen - royalty
I am, me.

I counted up my worth today
with the collection of wild hair,
bewildered imaginations,
and untamed personality
I rounded up 13 cents
Well, that's the number an MSN journalist gave me
between articles tallying up
unwarranted,
unrequited,
unredeemed deaths

and unnecessary,
un-relatable beauty tips
It's quite easy to feel - -
An "unable to put a finger on it" feeling
The articles,
they say that I am effortlessly targeted
and no one will fight for me
these media influences say
I am either riotous or scared
Whoever writing those articles
behind their safe,
guarded cubes,
those who have never shaken my hand
visited for Thanksgiving
ate my Gramma's banana pudding
read my poetry
want to make me fearful to leave my house.

I am not to be reckoned
unto classless buffoonery
I am to be revered
The stories you tell
of my people
lack the variety
that our skin easily reflects
Before you write your next article
knock on my door
drive up to my neighbors
have coffee with my mother
and we will all
tell you the truth

My Run-in With The Cops

In memory of Sandra Bland and the host of other victims slain during a "routine" stop

I didn't look like I was on drugs that night.

My mascara is runny. My dress is slightly tight. My wig looks frazzled. Yes. But, I'm not the hooker you thought I was. No, I was on the run. A speed chase. I, the rabbit. He, the horseman.
A mislead stranger drove opposite on the one-way street. He raced after me. I drove. Faster and faster. He chased me. In an unfamiliar part of town, I sped, and left turned, and u-turned. Until...until, I found the police officers.
Finally, my cavalry from this mysterious danger.

Cops! Please! Help me!
Well, what's the matter?
This man. Has been following ...
Well, why do you think he's following you?
Sir? I...I don't know.
Give me your license and registration.
But, sir, I didn't do anything wrong, I came to you for...
GET OUT OF THE CAR!
What did I do wrong?
GET OUT!

Barefoot on a wet sidewalk, face against grime encrusted brick wall, hands gathering at the small of my back. Quite naturally tears formulated, reminding me I was still human, and I was still right.
"WHY ARE YOU CRYING?!"
For a second, I wondered if this police officer really wanted to know why, or if he wanted to give me something to cry about. I came to you for help, and I'm the one against the wall with him, sitting comfortably in his car.

They said I was a drunk driver. I had nothing to drink that evening. They said my driving was dangerous. I was alone and needed to flee to safety. No matter the truth I told, there was always a response to make me a liar.

The New Black

is ripped jeans,
bold pink lips on plum skin
natural hair, twists, braids, bantu knots
bantu knot outs, braid outs, twist outs
shea butter, and EVOO
The new thought...new thought...new thought
breaking free from great grandma's
oppression
releasing ourselves from granddaddy's
segregated patterns
We now mix patterns
red jeans, blue polka dot top, denim jacket
bold colored Kenyan head wraps, maxi length
skirts
sports blazer, black denim, wingtip oxfords

The new black
is community
a quilted unity
open mics at cafes
reciting poems
sippin' shiraz, cabernet sauvignon
Discussing progression...progression
Learned lessons
forward moving sessions
by fireplaces
talkin' about how we matter
We now own homes...homes

Build homes
sell homes
obtaining degrees, we are the new brilliant
Africana Studies to learn ourselves
teach ourselves
grassroots taking over, for ourselves

The new black
answers to our ancestors prayers
we embrace ourselves
taking risks
because we want to…want to
chase dreams
because we have to…have to
no longer walk in fear

The New Black…new black…new black
don't stand down
don't back down
The New Black – strategic
innovative
investors
small business owners
large business owners
scholars
visionaries
social media gurus
poets
photographers
cartoonists
chefs

rulers
we live in etched concrete
we are books
Look up!
we stand over you
we are rewriting history to what we want it to say
we are catalysts to a post-racial America
we are elites, regal beings
the standard of beauty
laughter in the face of tragedy
always reemerging
resurfacing
resurrecting
you can't kill us
we are eternal

Sidekick

I firmly believe in what goes around comes around
the old reap what you sow
I know that famously feared witch
Karma exists
I often offer to be her Robin
pray for a faster return
on wrongful doers investments
or, for specific
embarrassing requests
like getting hit in the head
with a flying basketball
walk into an egg-shaped
force field of swarming gnats
step on a soaked bathroom mat at 3:47 am
let three eyelashes dive in your eye
when giving a speech
get caught on camera picking your nose
have diarrhea on a first date
walk into someone's fart
while yawning.

keep in mind when embarrassment comes for you
it was probably me who wished it for you

Battleship

In my circle run crazy women
crazy laughter,
crazy sense of self,
crazy confidence
That was her.
In her mouth rested
a roaring call to action
your strength couldn't stand
against her mighty
alpha way of being
her hair laid wildflowers
she let grow unattended
and her face
as supple as morning tea
But along came a season
that took it all away.

Life has a way of randomly
Choosing its victims of suffering.
Like the game of battleship,
a disease picked her row
her column
landed
anchor-heavy on her square.

Black women are the targets.
This thing hits 40 out of 100,000
the highest ratio of all womankind

a disease that fires
arrows at the lungs
cannons to the face
plants massive scars like trees
in places where high,
rosy cheeks
should be
a disease that makes your husband
reconsider his vows, her vows

We can't predict
what gifts life
will bring you.
There are some we
may not want
like Christmas socks,
but you can return the gift
but, my friend you can't return sarcoidosis.

She can't return
Grand Canyon grooves
and craters on her face
can't return
the plum-like plumpness
that gathers in her limbs
no matter the amount of sex
she can give,
her husband
won't come back

she can't return the disease

that changed the way she used to be
into a person, she can't look at in the mirror.

Band - aids

When we are asked the question,
How are you?
You are only to say
I am good
No one has time for a
not so good today answer
especially en route to work
in the checkout line
while pumping gas

If you have a moment
when you slip
and say you are
falling apart
tearing through
the net that is supposed to
hold you
if you have a second
of vulnerability
you may get the answer
it'll be alright
or
the most common
passive
avoidant band-aid
life goes on

there are times

when people do not know
what to say to ease
your pain
grief
and suffering
just rip the band-aid
that was poorly placed on you
replace it with a divine love
and a comfort from within

Wisdom Talk With Gramma #1
in setting boundaries

Me: Gramma, I was just being nice.
Gramma: Well, why don't you be nice to yourself?

God Bless The Periods!

My mom taught me periods are a blessing.
Many of us women tend to hold our tongue to
spare people's feelings.
But that one glorious week,
We unleash
every bit of buried thoughts
trampled opinions
suppressed reactions
when we were overlooked.
This is our time.
If you ever trespassed
in our off-season,
Gird your loins
Hold up your shields
we will take full advantage
to attack
by flushing out our mind,
spirit,
and cooch.

We Are Woman Enough

Dedicated to all women in the world, especially the amazing, phenomenal 13 from the "I Am Woman Enough" Campaign (empowerthewoman.com)

Women are deposit boxes filled with treasure the world withdraws from; treasures of wisdom, bravery, power, creativity, courage, validation, capability, liberation, love, worth, vibrancy, fullness, and wholeness.

Women are anointed to give plenty from empty hands.

We give a reason for the earth to spin. When we step down, kingdoms fall. When we rise, nations salute.

We are the driving force behind the wind, pushing everything into its rightful place.

We can work behind the scenes and on stage. Our flexibility is the only way things get done.

Do not sit us down.

Do not shut us up.

Our voices, our presence, our moving force will be felt. You will either respect us or get ran over. We are not the docile creatures you make us to be. Yet, we are gentle enough to allow a qualified man to lead. We are protectors, fighters, lovers, and light givers.

We are women enough.

Secret Life

I live a secret life
where I reunite
with my child-like mind
and wonder
just for a moment

moments lived in 15-minute increments
where I retreat
to the restroom
down the hall
and to the right,
to imagine
belt out songs
dance in the mirror
perform to an audience of 1.

For 15 minutes,
I am the superstar
I thought I'd always be
15 minutes
you can't touch me
15 minutes
I see strobes of rainbow colors
Spotlights tracing carefully each move
Amorous crowds screaming
my voice, like eternal seraphim
my body moves like the east coast, golden autumn
leaves

in the wind

When the timer ticks its end
and the lights begin to dim
I experience heart break
like the first time
all over again
I leave my beloved stage
and walk, sorrowfully,
to my cubicle

Angels

Angels spoke to me at seven years old
I told them about my day
the bullying,
the merciless revenge
the lonely
confusing
good times
they listened

on my porcelain throne
I was queen
This is where I met them
minutes entertaining
moments in tears and silence
rambles and riddles
they were my personal therapists

I imagined them
in all majestic glory
bathing in my empty tub
resting in my childish stories
sifting through an ancient Rolodex
of wise advice
to bestow upon me.
I meditated
before I knew what that was
and waited for their answers
an hour would pass

and I'd thank them
for traveling a days' length
just to talk to me
I'd say goodnight
and anxiously look forward
to talking tomorrow.

Train
a haiku
dedicated to those in "complicated" relationships

We're on the same train
to the same destination
just in different cars

Panties
a recount of my first date in college

Dating in college comes with more battle-wounds than victories. Your heart must never be on your sleeve or else you'll get heartbroken incessantly, and become bitter – like I did. Prepare for disastrous dates, empty flirtations, hopes up, and boundaries down. Hopefully, no one will ever experience anything like I did on my first date in college.

After dinner at IHOP, a collegiate's Grand Luxe Café, the guy (let's call him Donkey) dropped me off at my dorm. As I am preparing to get out of Donkey's car, he stops me and says, "Before you go, I just gotta ask one question." I anxiously wait as he presses the stereo knob. Dreading if he's going to ask me to kiss him, or play some cheesy, awkward slow jam from the 90s, in which I would be forced to kiss him. By this time, I've only kissed one guy. A flood of fear and insecurities bombarded my body – turning me into an awkward, stiff bodied girl.

But what happened next, I would've rather my fears come true. Snoop Dogg's voice sings loudly through fuzzy speakers, "Do you have a fresh pair of panties on?"

I think I died a short death but was resuscitated by anger.

Never With You

I'll never have the love with you
songs are made of
love the sun rises for,
just to see the earth's rounded smile
what kept maw maw and paw paw together
what had a man called Christ leave Heaven
just to go through hell for me

never with you

Social Media Killer

I'm not hip when it comes to phones. I still have a Samsung while everyone has an "i" everything. My wonderful antique phone has a cool trick I can do called swipe. With a swipe, I can text really fast by dragging my finger over the letters I want to use to build a word.

I was texting my Mother one day trying to say "social" media. However, my excitingly, ancient phone inserted "suicidal" media. I jerked and frantically backspaced before I accidently pressed "send," which would have had my Mother scrambling to gather an intervention crew. I probably should have pressed send, and let my Mother gather professionals because social media has killed me several times over.

Every day, I pour out the best of me on social media's plate for everyone to slice finely before chewing. "Likes," & "retweets" become the pat on the shoulder that affirms I've made a good career choice, if I look good that day, or chose a good mate. Silence is the killer that visits me in the evening to reflect upon my life. Approval is the driving force that keeps me pushing further in life just for someone to say that I've done well. Social Media is the vehicle I've willingly sat in without seatbelt and with wrecking abandon.

Home

Your arms are cedar doors
I willfully knock
hoping you'd open for me
Your eyes
made of lavender fields
inviting me
sweetly to your soul
Your chest
the roses you put forth
for me to lay and rest
Your fingers
flutter my skin
summon me to laughter
Your body
my dream home
southern and warm
I sit on your porch
every night
sow our wishes
onto fields of stars

Hey Little Black Girl

because everyone should write a letter to their younger self

Hey little black girl
with your two pigtails
totting a half-naked cabbage patch doll
I have something to tell you

Hey little caramel drop
with your old, butterscotch eyes
Eyes so old
your great-grandmother
probably gave them to you
I have something to tell you

Hey little ball of spunk
with your polka dot pants
striped shirt
the epitome of 4-year-old fashion
strutting your stuff
so confidently
I have something so important to tell you

I apologize

I made you grow up to be someone
I feared you'd become
I lost you

A heart full of spontaneity, humility,
a noble courage
fighting for your right
in a pool of wrong
you were bold by birthright
But this heart
Now cold as a plowing truck
on a Colorado acre
Still finds a way to beat
Still finds a way to exist
Hey little beautiful one
I'm sorry

I'm sorry I joined in with coward bullies
and called you names
to debilitate and weaken
I've let you down
Like countless broken promises
I've left you hanging like used towel rags
Never to be seen again until I'm dirty
And I'll expect you to clean up the mess

I've left you dry
An unattended garden
Weeds where roses once laid
Prickly where once smooth
Bare where once fruitful
I've watered everyone's lawn but your own
So yes
The grass is greener on the other brown girls' side
and it's my fault

I've been swayed by the tug o' wars
from everyone around me
without calling a truce
My sail moved by winds
of opinionated mouths;
I wasn't strong enough to
anchor myself in you
Your voice
Your dreams
Little girl, sweet girl
I've ignored your cries
left you bitter
sour faced full of lemons
I wonder if you can fix your mouth
to forgive me

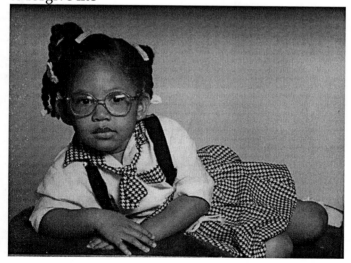

Polymath
a person of wide-ranging knowledge or learning

Many say I do too much
I am not focused
I say, there's much more to do.

I am told to do one thing
Be the best with that one thing
Focus on that *one* thing

What if you are good at more than one?
What happens to the young creative who enjoys
more?
What happens to me?

I say
It is never wrong to acquire
the lifestyle of a polymath
It is for the love of adventure
change
the maximization of potential
To never regret …
It is for the expression
of everything, I hold captive inside.

Love Is

love stands unwithered and broad-backed
when all else is fallen
believes and does not desire proof
a constant friend you could rely upon
a trusted ally
unwilling to betray
should you ever leave its side
love will leave the porch light on
every night
so you could find
your way home

Fall Back

I think people would rather pull back when they are hurting because it means safety. We would rather be alone than unsure if someone else would really care. It is never safe to be alone for long. Push back the tendencies to fall back. It is during these times that you must fall into relationships, fall into tearful vulnerabilities, fall into hope.

Questions I'd ask my 16-year-old daughter
and all other young women who may be in a rush to date

Who told you to open
and lift your bridges
to any boat, that approach your dock?
Don't you know
you must do a background check
before you let someone
lease your apartment?
Did you know
there's a reason
you conduct an interview
before you offer the job?
Did you know
that every application
doesn't get an offer to interview?
Did you know
these are the same questions
you must consider
before you remove the veil
to your sanctuary
or grant him
the silver toy key
to your flowered journal
that holds aged secrets.
A mishandled heart
may not recover quickly
if you adorn it
to someone unworthy

Standing Guard

Stand guard with me
adorn yourself in armor
mark time with shields
across hearts
forward march
resist forces
that rise against
our union
raise our cannons
swords
your back against mine
I with you
we will about-turn,
right and left incline
together
in sync
release fire into the dark
until it retreats
our flight of two
defending our grounds
when we've won
and lay our artillery
we will stand at ease
rest in arms
and revel in our triumph

ACKNOWLEDGEMENTS

Thank you, God, for being gracious enough to gift me with a heart for writing. Let this book be a reflection of obedience and grace.

Thank you to my Mother for being a true example of womanhood, femininity, and boldness. You always want the best for me, and I adore that.

Thank you, Gramma, for being the first poet I know. Although you have never written a poem, your life is pure poetry I am glad to read from daily.

Thank you, Auntie Pat, for your support and dependable honesty.

Thank you, Dad, for showing me how hard work really does lead to success.

Thank you to my sweet and dearest William (aka Booski). You are a real example of love and support. I am blessed to share this ride called life with you. You play a major role in me getting this book off of the ground. I will always cherish that. Thank you for writing a kick ass forward! You're the best writer I know.

Erica, thank you for your support. Watching you go hard for what YOU want has empowered me to do the same.

Daniela, thank you for helping me start this journey by providing so many tips, strategies, and hour-long conversations. I adore you.

Thank you, Angela Franklin, for the hour-long chats, empowering emails, motivating articles, and the TOUGH love. You have mentored me through this tedious, yet rewarding process. For that, I thank you wholeheartedly.

A ginormous Thank You to Hiram Sims, the originator of the Community Literature Initiative, and the facilitator for this dream. Thank you for making this dream real, tangible, and legendary.
Watching you chase and catch those dreams of yours inspired me greatly.

Thank you to my MASSIVE host of friends – You know who you are!!! If you don't, call me, I'll tell you.

I am eternally grateful for YOU, who is holding this book in your hands now. Thank you for your support. Because of you all, I now leave a legacy.

With gratitude,

Camari Carter

ABOUT THE AUTHOR

Camari Carter is an all around creative personality. She is a poet, blogger, photographer, natural hair stylist, pianist, and singer. Camari is passionate about business, social justice, and the arts. Camari would describe her writing as evocative, painful, yet triumphant and witty. Her photography is loaded with color, beauty, and warmth. She is drawn to create art that pierces the heart.

Carter received her Bachelors of Art in Political Science and Masters in Organizational Management. She intends to rock the world with her words, art, and mind. She currently resides in Los Angeles, CA.

For more info, visit <u>www.camaricarter.com</u>
or follow Camari on all Social Media Platforms.

Instagram: @camaricarter
Twitter: @camaricarter
Periscope: @camaricarter
Snapchat: @moonpower
Facebook: Camari Carter

World Stage Press
Verse from the Village

To support the creation and proliferation of African
American Literature, please become a supporting
member by visiting www.worldstagepress.org